Taste of Guyana!

Authentic Guyanese Recipes for Every Kitchen

Marcus Ramsarran

WORKBOOK PRESS LLC
187 E Warm Springs Rd,
Suite B285 Las Vegas NV 89119 USA

Website: https://workbookpress.com/
Hotline: 1-888-818-4856
Email: admin@workbookpress.com

Ordering Information:
Quantity sales. Special discounts are available on quantity purchases by corporations, associations, and others. For details, contact the publisher at the address above.

Library of Congress Control Number:
ISBN-13:   978-1-965732-85-4   Paperback Version

REV. DATE: 09/10/2025

Taste of Guyana!

Authentic Guyanese Recipes for Every Kitchen

by

MARCUS RAMSARRAN

Introduction

Welcome to Taste of Guyana, a celebration of the vibrant flavors, rich history, and soulful spirit of Guyanese cuisine. Nestled on the northern coast of South America, Guyana is a melting pot of cultures — African, Indian, Indigenous, Portuguese, Chinese, and European — each adding their own unique touch to the nation's food traditions. The result is a culinary landscape as diverse and colorful as its people.

In this cookbook, you'll discover cherished family recipes passed down through generations, street food favorites bursting with bold spices, and festive dishes reserved for special holidays and gatherings. From the smoky aroma of pepperpot to the comforting warmth of dhal and rice, every page invites you into a kitchen filled with stories, memories, and love.

Whether you're a proud Guyanese reconnecting with your roots or a curious cook eager to explore new flavors, Taste of Guyana offers more than just recipes — it offers a piece of home. So roll up your sleeves, gather your ingredients, and let the journey begin. Welcome to the taste of tradition. Welcome to the Taste of Guyana!

Channa & Potato Curry

Channa & Potato Curry is a popular Vegetarian Dish throughout the Caribbean but mostly popular in the Indian culture in Guyana and is most often Served at Hindu Religious functions in Guyana. Particularly at Indian Weddings and is part of other dishes known as "Seven Curry"!

Ingredients

- 1/2 lb. Dried Channa or 1 tin of Channa (Chickpea)
- 4 potatoes, peeled and chopped
- 2 cloves garlic, chopped
- 1 small onion Chopped
- 2 wiri (Thai red/green) peppers finely chopped
- 2tbsp Curry powder
- 1/2 tsp Gheera
- 1/2 Tsp Masala
- 1/2 Tsp Salt or Salt to taste

Instructions

If Dried Channa is used, Pressure Cook the channa in salted water (1 tsp) for later use

Wash and peel potatoes then chop them.

Heat oil and add onion and Garlic.

Add the Curry and Cook until almost Dry.

Add Potato and Green Seasonings. Stir until Coasted with curry.

Add Channa and Mix. Then add the pepper

Add the Salted Channa Water. Pour enough to almost cover the channa & potato (about 2 cups)

Cook until potatoes are tender and Mixture is Thick

Season with Salt, Gheera, Masala. Add pepper to taste.

Split Peas Cook-up

Split Peas Cook-up is a savoury rice dish made with split peas (lentils) and assorted meat.

Ingredients

- 3 cups parboiled rice
- 1cup uncooked split peas
- 8 pieces pigtail (soaked for approx. 1 hr) (Optional)
- 2 lbs Beef (Cubed) (Also Optional, omit all meat if you are Vegan)
- 1 large onion, chopped
- 3 cloves garlic, peeled and halved
- Fresh seasoning – chive, thyme, shadon beni, chopped finely
- Large pinch of black pepper
- 1 oz butter

Instructions

Wash rice and set aside.

Wash peas and put to cook in water over medium high heat with pig tail and garlic until peas can be crushed but not too soft.

Brown Beef

Add chopped onion, chives, thyme etc. which has been cut up finely and also black pepper.

After approx. 5-10 minutes add rice and butter, turn down heat, cover pot. When water has been absorbed (say 5 minutes) stir and add a little water covering tightly. Turn heat to low and let rice simmer until cooked approx. 15 minutes. You may add a little water the 2nd time if required.

Fluff the rice with a fork and adjust seasoning if necessary. Serve.

Callaloo Cook-up Rice

Callaloo cook-up Rice is a one-pot rice dish that consists of rice, a variety of meats, and fresh herbs that is cooked with coconut milk and callaloo.

Ingredients

- 1/2 lb Pickled pig's tail (1 large-tail) or pig's foot (optional)
- 1 lb Beef stew meat, cubed
- 2 tb Oil
- 1/2 lb Raw tripe *
- 5 c Water
- 1 md Onion, peeled and chopped
- 2 Garlic cloves, peeled and chopped
- 1 lb Calalloo (Spinach) leaves, chopped (see-note)
- 1/4 ts Chopped fresh Habanero-(Scotch Bonnet) pepper **
- 5 Ounce can coconut milk
- Salt and pepper
- 1 lb long-grain rice
- 1/2 c Chopped red bell pepper,for garnish * (may substitute chicken)

Instructions

Put the pig's tail in pot and cover with water; bring to a boil, and boil for 1 hour. Drain and set aside. Brown beef in oil, then add tripe and water. Bring to a boil, reduce heat and cook at a gentle boil for about 1 hour. Add pig's tail and cook until liquid has reduced to about 3 cups. Cut tripe into pieces and cut meat from pig's foot; return meats to pot. Add onion, garlic, taro leaves, Habanero, coconut milk and salt and pepper to taste. Simmer for 10 minutes. Add rice. Cover the pot, reduce the heat and simmer for about 30 minutes, until mixture looks nice and green. Garnish with chopped red pepper.

Chowmein

Chowmein is a popular noodle dish in Guyanese cuisine and is given to us by the Guyanese people of Chinese descent. Chinese cuisine has an important place in Guyanese food culture as there are many wonderful ingredients and products that we use to make our food, our food. Over time we have adjusted flavors and sourced local ingredients to make it our own unique fusion.

Ingredients

- 12oz package dried chowmein noodles
- water for boiling
- 1 tbsp vegetable oil + 1 tsp salt for water
- 2 tbsp sesame oil
- 1/2 tsp black pepper
- 1/2 tsp Chinese five spice powder
- 1 tsp garlic powder
- 1/2 tsp salt
- For chicken (can be seasoned hours before or overnight)
- 2-3lbs cut up chicken breasts or other desired protein
- 1 tbsp olive oil, for marinade
- 3 tsp reduced sodium soy sauce
- 1 tbsp casareep or browning sauce
- 2 tbsp green seasoning
- dash of salt
- 1 tbsp olive oil, to cook chicken

For vegetables

- 1-2 stalks bak choy or 1 cup cabbage, cut into strips
- 1 cup pre-shredded or julienned carrots
- 10-12 Chinese long beans (bora bean)
- 1/2 red bell pepper, cut into strips
- 3 tbsp reduced sodium soy sauce
- 1 tbsp sesame oil
- 1/4 cup water
- 1 tbsp oyster sauce
- 1 tsp freshly grated ginger
- 2 stems scallion, sliced
- wiri wiri or scotch bonnet pepper, optional

Instructions

Season chicken with olive oil, soy sauce, casareep, green seasoning, and salt. Set aside.

Prep vegetables, grate ginger, and set aside.

Bring large pot of water to a boil with salt and oil. Add chowmein noodles, cook according to package directions.

Drain noodles in colander, rinse immediately with cold water. Spread noodles out in an aluminum pan or long shallow pan.

Season noodles with sesame oil, black pepper, Chinese five spice, garlic powder, and salt. Set aside.

Sauté chicken 8-10 minutes until most liquid has evaporated, set aside when done.

Cook vegetables in a heavy-bottom pot or wok, add soy sauce, sesame oil, water, oyster sauce, grated ginger, and pepper let simmer for 30 seconds. Add vegetables and cook for 3-4 minutes.

Turn heat off, add seasoned chowmein noodles to pot with vegetables and toss in chicken. Add scallions and mix thoroughly. Adjust salt to taste.

Chicken Low Mein

low mein noodles are usually stirred with a sauce made from soy sauce and other seasonings. Vegetables such as bok choy and cabbage can be mixed in and meats like roast pork, beef or chicken are often added.

Ingredients:

- 1 (4) lb chicken cut into 16 pieces
- 1 tbsp freshly grated ginger
- 1 tbsp cornstarch
- 1 tbsp hoisin sauce
- 1 tbsp sesame oil
- 3 tbsp Chinese rice wine
- 2 tbsp soy sauce
- 1 tsp white pepper
- 1 tbsp garlic paste
- 1 tsp five spice powderPrep for Chicken:
- Wash and pat chicken pieces until dry, and set aside
- In a bowl mix all other ingredients well
- Combine this mixture with the chicken pieces

Assembly of Noodles

- 1 lb of Chinese noodles
- ½ lb of bora (Chinese long bean) cut in 2″ pieces
- 2 medium carrots sliced into thin rounds
- 3 bunches of Chinese greens, chopped coarsely
- 1 cup of finely shredded cabbage
- 3 tbsp soy sauce
- 2 chicken bouillons
- ½ tsp white pepper
- 6 blades of finely sliced scallion
- 1 large white onion chopped
- 3 wiri wiri peppers minced(optional)
- 5 tbsp vegetable oi l
- 1/4 cup of water
- ½ tsp five spice powder

Preparation

Boil, cook, and drain noodles Set aside

In a wok, add 3 tbsp vegetable oil

Heat on a high flame, add chicken pieces

Cook until all liquid is absorbed and chicken is browned

Remove chicken and set aside

Add 2 tbsp vegetable oil to the wok

Toss in onions, bora, and carrots and cook for 2 minutes on high heat

Add bouillons and water and continue to cook until water is almost absorbed

Add cabbage, wiri wiri pepper, and Chinese greens, and cook for 1 minute

Return chicken to pot, and add noodles, soy sauce, and white pepper, and five spice powder

Mix well and top with chopped scallions

** Variations: If you cannot get wiri wiri peppers, use scotch bonnet, the flavors assume a great place in this dish. In addition I use baby string beans in lieu of bora (also known as Chinese long bean)

Cook-up Rice

Ingredients

- 1 cup parboiled rice
- 1 lb black eye peas
- 1 lb chicken or beef
- 1 onion (chipped)
- 2 cloves garlic (chipped)
- 2 tbsp soya sauce
- 1 coconut or coconut milk
- 1½ cups of water
- 6 okras (optional)
- 1 tbsp cooking oil
- Salt and hot pepper to taste
- 1 chicken bullion cube
- Thyme
- Sprinkle of black-pepper

Preparation

Soak black eye peas overnight.

Grate coconut; add water to grated coconut.

Squeeze grated coconut in the water. Strain the mixture, and pour the white liquid (coconut milk) in cooking pot.

Cut up the chicken and season it with salt, black-pepper and soy sauce.

Fry chicken for about 5 minutes in oil.

Wash rice and add to the pot with coconut milk.

Add soaked black eye peas.

Add fried chicken.

Add bullion cube, thyme, onion, garlic and whole okras.

Add salt and pepper to taste.

Cover pot and cook with medium heat for about 40 minutes until rice is soft and liquid is absorbed.

Garnish with chipped shallot blades.

Salted fish

Ingredients

- 1 lb of salted snapper (or your favourite brand/type of salted fish)
- 3 tbsp Oil
- 1 cup of diced tomatoes
- 1 chopped medium onion
- 3 cloves of minced garlic
- 1 chopped wi-ri wi-ri pepper (optional)
- 1/2 cup chopped eschallot
- 1/2 cup chopped Celery

Preparation

Bring a large pot of water to a rapid boil.

Add saltfish and boil for half an hour.

if you wish your saltfish to be less salty, drain and Place salted fish back in boiling water for another 5 minutes

When saltfish is done, drain and loosen with fork (or clean fingers) until all the pieces are completely broken up. There should be no clumps.

Heat oil in a medium frying pan.

In frying pan, add garlic, onion, and pepper. Fry for about 3 minutes or until onions are soft.

Add saltfish for another 4,

Add tomatoes and eschalot

Fry until all the water from the tomatoes is gone.

Stir constantly.

Chicken Curry/Curry Chicken

Chicken curry is a common delicacy in South Asia, Southeast Asia, as well as in the Caribbean (where it is usually referred to as "curry chicken").

Ingredients

- 3 lb chicken cut up into small pieces
- 4 medium potatoes, peeled and halved
- 1 whole garlic
- 1 small hot pepper
- 2 medium onions
- 2 tbsp oil
- 2 tbsp ground curry powder
- ½ tbsp gharam Massala
- 1 piece cinnamon stick

Preparation

Grind garlic, one onion, and pepper

Heat oil in stew pan.

Add mixture of ground garlic, pepper and onion, gharam massala and curry powder.

Allow to fry on slow heat for about 3 to 4 minutes.

Add chicken and potatoes and salt to taste.

Add cinnamon stick.

Cook on slow heat for 15 to 20 minutes.

Add one cup of water and sprinkle one chipped onion. Bring to boil for about 20 minutes until potatoes are fully cooked.

Note: Curried beef or lamb may be prepared in a similar manner.

Bhunjal Chicken (special way)

Bhunjal chicken is basically the dried down version of curry. When you fry the chicken in the curry paste, let it cook in its own liquid. In other words, cover the pot and let it sweat. Then when the water starts to dry out take off the cover.

It is important to use lots of oil to do this. After cooking skim the oil off.

Crab Curry

This delicious dish is called Crab curry and is made with coconut milk also Curry Sauce/paste. It's a treat for your tastebuds and takes you back to child hood.

Ingredients

- 1/2 cup water
- 2 limes, juice of
- 2 tablespoons ginger
- 2 tablespoons garlic
- 6 large crabs (cleaned)
- 1 1/2 cups coconut milk
- 3 tablespoons cooking oil
- 3 tablespoons curry powder
- 1 teaspoon salt, chive, thyme
- pepper

Instructions

Cut the crabs in small pieces and use the lime juice for washing them. Use the ginger, minced chive, garlic, thyme to season the crabs. Pour the oil into a preheated pot.

Make a paste by mixing the curry, salt and the pepper and add it to the hot oil. Next add the crab meat along with the coconut milk when the mixture thickens.

Next allow the curry crabs to simmer for about 25 minute covered. When the curry crabs are done serve them with cassava dumplings,rice or roti.

Pepperpot

This dish develops more flavour when left over a period of days. It must be reheated o boiling point each day. This is a typical Amerindian dish.

Ingredients

- 3 lbs of meat- beef, lamb, pork, goat or chicken
- 1 cup cassareep
- 4-5 cinnamon sticks (not ground)
- 1 1/2 inch orange peel
- 6-8 cloves
- 1-2 wiri wiri peppers
- 1/2- 3/4 cup brown sugar
- 1 1/2 tsp salt
- 16 cups water

Instructions

Steam the meat for about 15 minutes so that all the fat can be removed. Once you have steamed the meat, remove any dangling pieces of fat. Discard the liquid in the pot.

In another large pot, add meat, cassareep, and all other ingredients. Add the water and boil until the meat is tender and until the broth has reduced by three-quarters, a few hours. My dad usually boils the meat until it falls off the bones, but some people like their pepperpot meat a bit more on the tough side. It's all about preference.

Adjust salt to suit your tastes.

Pepperpot is best when made a couple days ahead.

How to steam the meat

Place meat in a pot with enough water to cover just 1/4 way up the pot. Let meat simmer on low heat until the fat congeals and can be removed from each piece, about 15 minutes. Remember, you are not cooking the meat during this step, just heating the meat enough so the fat can be removed. This allows for a lean stew.

Pepperpot does not need to refrigerate and can be stored on the stove top. Flavor is best when made a few days ahead.

Hassar Curry

Hassar curry is a common delicacy made in the Caribbean using many different spices including curry powder.

Ingredients

- 6 hassars
- 1 or 2 onions
- 1 oz curry powder (or massala)
- 4 – 6 wirri-wirri peppers
- 2 cloves garlic
- 2 tbsp cooking oil
- Salt
- Lime juice or vinegar
- ½ oz margarine
- 1 cup coconut milk

Instructions

Wash, clean and salt the hassars, and set aside for about one hour. Do not remove the shells. Afterwards, rinse and dry the hassars.

Prepare the curry sauce as follows: heat 2 teaspoons of oil, and cook the onion and garlic lightly (do not brown). Add curry powder blended with 3 – 4 tablespoons of water. Add 1 cup water or coconut milk and stir.

Put the hassars into the curry sauce.

Add the lime juice and leave to cook for 15 – 20 minutes until the sauce is thick, adding more water if necessary.

When finished, put the hassars onto a dish and pour the curry sauce over.

The shells may be removed before serving.

Shrimp Curry

Guyanese style shrimp curry is a savory curry made with traditional Indian spices with a Caribbean flare.

Ingredients

- 1 lb shrimp or as needed
- 1 tbsp oil
- 1 onion
- 3 cloves garlic
- 2 bay leaves
- 2 tsp gheera (roasted ground cumin and coriander found in west indian stores)
- 2 tsp turmeric
- 1 tbsp curry powder
- Salt to taste
- Pepper to taste
- 2 tbsp grated coconut, optional
- 1 can coconut milk
- 1 tomato cut into 8ths
- 1/2 cup cilantro

Preparation

Optional: Marinate shrimp for 2 or more hours in fridge with lime juice and 1/2 tbsp curry powder.

Chop the onions, heat the oil in a pan and fry lightly with bay leaves after a few minutes add garlic, so that garlic don't burn

Add the turmeric, curry powder and gheera and fry for a minute then add 1/2 cup of water to keep from burning.

Add the shrimp and grated coconut, salt and pepper, fry for a few more minutes.

Add coconut milk, stir and cover the pot. Boil on medium heat until shrimp is cooked and liquid has boiled down into a creamy sauce, about 5 minutes.

Lastly add tomato before removing from the heat.

Serve hot with rice, sprinkled with grated coconut and cilantro !!

Katahar Curry

Katahar curry is a delicious Dish cooked in coconut Milk and Curry p0wder.

Ingredients

- 2 medium katahar cleaned
- milk extracted from 1 grated dried coconut
- 1 teaspoon ground turmeric(dye)
- 3 tablespoons garam masala
- 3 tablespoon ground jeera
- 2 whole cloves
- 1 inch piece cinnamon
- 1 large tomato,chopped
- 1 large onion, chopped
- 5 flakes garlic, chopped
- 2 wiri wiri pepper(any pepper of your choice)
- 1 tablespoon oil
- Salt to taste.

Instructions

Wash the already cleaned katahar thoroughly in a colander.Drain.

Heat the oil in a karahi/deep pot.

Add the cinnamon and cloves.

Add the drained katahar and stir until coated with oil.Reduce flame to slow.

Add salt and stir.

Add the turmeric, stir until all the katahar is coated.Fry for 1 minute.

Add the garam masala, stir again and fry for 1 minute.

Add the jeera,stir for 1 minute.

Add the coconut milk, stir. The milk should cover the katahar.

Turn up the flame until it starts to boil then reduce it back to medium.

Add the chopped tomato.

Cover the pot and allow to cook until all the seeds are cooked.

It tastes best when it is dried-down/cooked down completely and oil starts to come out.Serve with dal and rice(7 curries) or with hot sada or paratha rotis.

Egg Curry

Egg is a versatile cooking ingredient. Many people who do not eat meat eat eggs. Delicious and quick this curry can be ready in 25 minutes.

Ingredients

- 4 boiled eggs or as needed
- 1/2 onion sliced
- 2 cloves garlic sliced thin (or crushed)
- 1/2 tomato sliced
- 1/2 teaspoon curry powder
- 1 scallion
- dash of black pepper
- 1/4 hot pepper (I used habanero)
- 1 tablespoon vegetable oil
- 1/2 cup water
- salt to taste (less than 1/4 teaspoon)

Instructions

Prepare the onion, hot pepper, garlic, scallion and tomato and set aside.

Put the eggs to boil on a medium to high flame (cover eggs with cold water and bring to a boil), then as soon as it comes to a vigorous boil, turn off the heat, cover the pot and let it stand in there for 10-12 minutes.

Heat the oil in a sauce pan on medium/high heat, then add the sliced onion and garlic and allow to cook for a few minutes. Until they go soft, release their aromatic oils and stars to brown on the edges. Then turn down the heat to medium /low and add the curry powder and slices of hot pepper (if you need some good madras curry powder, check out the store – where you can find tons of Caribbean goodies) and stir. Allow this to cook for about 3-4 minutes, so the curry won't have a "raw" taste to it.

The next step is to add the water and give it a good stir and bring it up to a gentle simmer. Then add the slices of tomato and scallion and top off with the eggs. Cut the eggs in half before adding and be very gentle at this point forward, since the eggs will fall apart easily. Add the salt and black pepper at this point as well.

On low heat, cover the pot and allow to cook for abut 4-5 minutes, so the sauce thickens and all the flavors get a chance to marry together. If you find that the sauce is a bit runny, cook for an extra minute or two with the pot uncovered.

Serve with Rice,Quinoa or Roti

Bora with Shrimp

Bora (or Chinese long bean) is used in many Guyanese dishes including Fried rice and chowmein. It's mostly used stir Fried with beef, chicken or shrimp.

Ingredients

- 1lb bora beans
- 1 small yellow onion
- 3 garlic cloves
- 1 wiri wiri pepper or scotch bonnet
- 1 large tomato
- 2 small potatoes or 1 Idaho
- 1 large chicken/vegetable bouillon cube or 3 small cubes
- Dash of black pepper
- 3 tbsp canola or olive oil
- 1/3 cup water
- Desired protein – shrimp, chicken, beef, saltfish

Instructions

Chop heads off of beans and cut into one inch pieces. Rinse chopped beans and set aside.

Gather all ingredients. Chop onion, garlic, tomato, potatoes, and pepper (if you don't want this too spicy don't chop the pepper). I like this dish spicy so I added two wiri wiri peppers, chopped.

Prep and season whichever protein you will be using, set aside. I used two handfuls of white belly shrimp and seasoned it like this.

Heat a caharee or pot with 3 tbsp oil. Add garlic, onions, and pepper. Allow to saute until onions become tender. Add tomatoes.

Once tomatoes are soft and looks like a sauce, add chopped bora. Let cook for 5-6 minutes then add bouillon cube, black pepper and water. Stir and let cook for 20-25 minutes.

After 20 minutes, add the potatoes, let cook for 15-20 minutes.

While potatoes cook, cook your protein separately and set aside. If using beef, chicken or saltfish, you may want to cook this earlier on before cooking the bora.

Once potatoes are cooked, add your cooked protein and mix to incorporate the flavors.

Enjoy with rice, roti, or even bakes!

Duck Curry

Ingredients

- 2 ½ lbs skinless duck thighs cut in half
- Juice of 1 lime
- 3 cloves garlic, crushed
- 5 sprigs thyme
- 1 Thai chili pepper

- 3 scallions finely chopped
- 1 medium onion finely chopped
- 1 tsp salt
- 1 chicken bouillon
- 3 tbsp canola oil

Curry Paste

- ¼ cup curry powder
- ¼ tsp cumin
- ¼ tsp garam masala

- 3 cloves garlic crushed
- 5 sprigs thyme
- About 3 tbsp water

Preparation

Place duck in a bowl with enough water to cover and juice of 1 lime; rinse. Add garlic, thyme, scallion, chili pepper and salt to duck. Let marinate for at least an hour.

To make curry paste, add curry powder, cumin, garam masala, garlic, thyme and water; mix. In a deep frying pan over medium heat, add canola oil. When oil is hot, add curry paste and onion. Cook for 7-10 minutes, stirring frequently. Add seasoned duck to pot and stir to coat. Cook for 15 minutes, without adding any liquid. After 15 minutes, add enough water to cover duck; add the bouillon also. Bring to a boil, then lower heat. Cook for an additional 30 minutes or until duck is tender. When duck is tender, remove from heat and garnish with chopped scallion. Serve over rice or with a hot roti.

Lamb Curry

Ingredients

- 3lbs lamb meat
- Pre-season for meat
- 2 tbsp green seasoning
- 1/2 tsp garam masala
- 1/2 tsp geera (roasted cumin)
- 1 tsp madras curry powder
- Curry Paste
- 2 tbsp green Seasoning
- 2 tbsp garam masala
- 2 1/2 tbsp madras curry powder
- 1 heaping tsp tomato paste
- 3 tbsp water to mix (more if needed)
- Remaining Ingredients
- 3 tbsp canola oil
- 4-5 curry leaves
- 1/2 yellow onion, sliced
- 5-6 cloves
- 1 small cinnamon stick
- Salt to taste (start with 1 1/2 tsp)
- Boiling water on reserve in kettle
- 2 medium potatoes, peeled and quartered

Instructions

Wash and clean meat then chop into 3in chunks. See note below on washing.

Season meat with pre-seasoning, let marinate overnight or a few hours.

Prep ingredients. Make curry paste, set aside. Gather remaining ingredients, set aside.

Heat 3 tbsp oil in karahi or heavy bottom pot. Add curry leaves and fry until fragrant and brown. Add curry paste mixture. Saute mixture until medium brown. Add meat, toss meat with curry paste mixture to coat. Add sliced onion, cloves, cinnamon stick, and salt. Bounjal the meat -Let meat cook in its own liquid until it has evaporated and curry paste has seared onto meat, about 20-25 minutes.

Pour boiling water over meat, enough to cover the meat. Let meat boil until tender, adding a little water at a time throughout the process until meat is tender, about 45 minutes or more.

Add potatoes once meat is almost tender. Remove curry from heat once potato is cooked. Adjust salt to taste.

Mutton/Goat curry

Ingredients

- 4lbs goat meat, chopped, shoulder or leg
- Pre-season
- 3 tbsp green Seasoning
- 1 tbsp madras curry powder
- 1 tsp geera (ground, roasted cumin)
- 1 tsp garam masala
- Curry paste mixture
- 2 tbsp + 1 tsp garam masala, heaping
- 3 tbsp madras curry powder, heaping
- 4 tbsp green Seasoning
- 4 tbsp water to make paste
- Remaining Ingredients
- 2 tbsp dried thyme or 4 sprigs fresh thyme leaves
- 1 tsp all spice, ground
- 1/4 tsp five spice, ground
- 10-15 cloves
- 1 stick cinnamon bark (not ground)
- 1/2 onion, sliced
- 3 sprigs scallions, finely chopped
- 2-3 wiri wiri peppers or 1 scotch bonnet
- 1 tbsp tomato paste
- 6 curry leaves - burn in oil before adding masala mixture
- 2 tsp salt, add more to suit taste
- 2 medium potatoes, quartered
- 5 tbsp canola or vegetable oil for sautéing curry paste
- Boiling water

Instructions

Clean and chop meat. Wash meat according to preference.

Season meat with pre-seasoning, let marinate overnight or a few hours

Prep ingredients. Make curry paste, set aside. Gather spices, onions and scallions, pepper, set aside

Heat 5 tbsp oil in karahi or heavy bottom pot. Add curry leaves and fry until fragrant and brown. Add curry paste mixture. Sauté mixture until medium brown. Add meat, toss meat with curry paste mixture to coat. Let meat cook in its own liquid until it has evaporated and curry paste has seared onto meat, about 20-25 minutes.

Add salt, dry spices, thyme, cinnamon bark, sliced onions, scallions. Toss to combine.

Pour boiling water over meat, enough to cover the meat. Add tomato paste. Let meat boil until tender, adding a little water at a time throughout the process until meat is cooked, about 2-3 hours.

Add potatoes once meat is almost tender. Remove curry from heat once potato is cooked.

If using a pressure cooker, after step 5, remove meat and liquid and transfer to a pressure cooker. See note above under "Pressure cooker" on cooking directions.

Guyanese Style Fried Rice

Ingredients

- 1 3/4 cup extra-long grain white rice
- 1 cup diced carrots
- 1 cup chopped bora beans (Chinese long beans)
- 1 cup shredded cabbage
- ¼ cup yellow onion, finely diced
- 2 cloves garlic, crushed
- 3-4 scallion sprigs, finely sliced
- 1 tsp mushroom sauce
- 4 tbsp dark soy sauce
- 2 tsp oyster sauce
- 1 tsp freshly grated ginger
- ½ tsp Chinese five spice
- 5 tbsp vegetable or canola oil
- Salt, as needed
- Meat

- seasoned hours before or overnight
- 2-3lbs cut up chicken breasts or other desired protein (beef, pork, etc..)
- 1 tbsp olive oil, for marinade
- 3 tsp reduced sodium soy sauce
- 1 tbsp cassareep or browning sauce
- 2 tbsp green seasoning
- dash of salt
- 1 tbsp olive oil, to cook chicken

Directions

Cook rice according to package directions. Spread in a long shallow pan. Let cool overnight or for a couple of hours. Rice should be completely cold.

Cook chicken and set aside.

Chop and prep all vegetables Combine mushroom sauce, soy sauce, and oyster sauce in one bowl set aside.

In a wok or Kalahari sauté onions, garlic, and ginger in 1 tbsp oil until onions are tender, 1-2 minutes.

Add 1 tbsp oil to the pan then add carrots, sauté a few minutes. Push carrots aside, add 3 tbsp oil then add bora and cabbage together. Sauté 1-2 minutes.

Add rice a little at a time tossing with vegetables. Add sauce mixture and Chinese five spice. Fry the rice until completely covered with sauce.

Toss in the chicken and scallions.

Soups

Fish Broth

Ingredients

- fish or fish head, about ¾ lb
- 1 qt cold water
- 1 onion
- 2 tbsp butter
- 1 lb Ground provisions root vegetables
- ½ tsp salt
- ¼ tsp black pepper
- Eschallot
- celery
- 1 clove

Preparation

Cut up the onion, eschallot and celery and lightly fry together in the butter. Avoid browning and use a cover if necessary.

Clean and add the fish or fish head, water and salt. Heat to boiling.

Skim and add the vegetables, previously peeled, washed and diced. Add the clove, reduce the heat and simmer for 30 – 40 minutes.

Remove the fish, separate the flesh from the bone, return the flesh to the soup and reheat.

Remove the fish head, if used, and serve it separately, if desired. Garnish with chopped parsley and serve hot.

Metemgee Soup

Metemgee is a Guyanese Creole "Stew" of mixed meat, salt fish, and dumplings with coconut milk, cassava, yam, plantains, okra, onions, thyme, and hot pepper sauce.

Ingredients

- 6 ounces Beef, cubed (optional)
- 6 ounces pork or Salted Beef cubed (Optional)
- 8 oz salt-fish
- 2 cups chicken stock (or water)
- 2 cups coconut milk
- 1 pound sweet potato, peeled, cubed
- 1 pound yam, peeled, cubed
- 1 pound plantain, peeled, cubed
- 1 teaspoon fresh thyme, finely chopped
- 2 habanero, seeded, finely chopped
- 1 red onion, cut into rings
- 1 pound okra, sliced
- 1 cup flour
- 2 tablespoons butter, small cubes
- 1 teaspoon baking powder
- ½ teaspoon salt
- 2 tablespoons sugar
- 2 tablespoons Water

Instructions

Dust beef and pork with flour and sauté.

Soak salt fish in warm water for about 15 minutes. Drain. Remove skin and bones.

Discard. Squeeze fish dry.

Grate the coconut, pour one pint of water over, squeeze well and strain to extract the coconut milk. Arrange peeled plantains and seasonings in layers over the meat, with salt fish on top.

Add coconut milk and cook, covered, until almost tender, about 30 minutes.

Place onions and okras on top of salt fish. Steam, covered, for 10 minutes.

Add dumplings and steam for another 8 minutes.

For the Dumplings

Rub flour and butter together. Add baking powder, salt, and sugar. Add enough of the water to make a stiff dough.

Chicken Soup

Ingredients

- 3 large chicken bouillon cubes (if you have small ones, use 6 cubes)
- 1 tsp black pepper
- 1 tsp salt
- 5 cloves of garlic
- 1 onion
- 1 gallon of water (16 cups)
- 1/4 cup yellow split peas (not pictured)
- 2 skinny cassava chopped into 2 inch pieces (I say skinny b/c the thicker ones
- are just harder to peel)
- 4-5 eddoes chopped in half or quarters if you bought large ones (4-5 is about 1/2 lb)
- 1/2 lb pumpkin chopped into 4 in pieces
- 2 cups chopped fresh spinach (1 cup if using frozen spinach)
- 1 green plantain chopped in 1 1/2 inch pieces
- 2 bay leaves
- 2 red scotch bonnet peppers or 3 wiri wiri peppers
- 2 lbs chicken cleaned and chopped in medium size pieces
- 1 tsp black pepper
- 1 tsp cayenne pepper
- 1 tbsp casareep or browning sauce

For Dumpling

- 3/4 cup flour
- 1/2 tsp baking powder
- 1/2 tsp salt
- 1/4 tsp black pepper
- 1tbsp butter, (not pictured)
- 1/4 cup whole milk

Instructions

Clean, chop, and season the chicken, set aside

Pour 16 cups of water into a large deep pot and bring to a boil.

After peeling, wash cassava, eddoes, and plantain, set aside.

Rinse and chop spinach, pumpkin, onion garlic and scotch bonnet then put into boiling water with 1/4 cup washed split peas. Cover with lid, reduce heat to medium, and continue to boil for 40 minutes.

Use pot spoon to mash the pumpkin on the side of the pot to see if it is soft. The peas should also be soft, if it is not, continue to boil until it is almost disappearing into the soup.

Once peas are soft add the plantains, cassava, and eddoes along with 3 bouillon cubes, and bay leaves.

If you feel this needs more water you can add another 2 cups at this point.

Turn the heat to low-medium and let the vegetables cook for another 20 minutes until they are medium-soft.

While the vegetables are cooking, make the dough for the dumpling (it will be a stiff dough which is okay.

Cook the chicken in a separate pan in 1 tbsp of oil. Sauté until the chicken is cooked and browned.

Once the eddoes, cassava, and plantains are cooked through, add the chicken to the soup. Let the flavors simmer together on low heat for 15 minutes. Give it a good stir.

Break small pieces of dumpling dough and drop it into the soup. The dumplings will cook in approximately 5 minutes. Stir the soup as your drop the dumplings in.

Let it simmer for an additional 10 minutes.

Corn Soup

Ingredients

- 1 large onion
- 3 garlic cloves
- 1 celery stalk
- 1 cup corn kernels
- 1/4 cup diced carrot
- 1/4 cup diced red pepper
- 1/4 cup diced green pepper
- 1/3 cup yellow split peas
- Scotch bonnet pepper (optional)
- 4 tbsp salted butter
- 1 tsp salt
- 1 tsp black pepper
- 2 sprigs parsley
- 1 sprig thyme
- 3 cups water (for base)
- 1 1/2 cups coconut milk

- 4 cups water (for use after pureeing base)
- 1 tsp salt or 1 small bouillon cube
- 1 tsp black pepper
- 2 green plantains

- 1/4 cup diced carrots
- Corn kernels
- 6-8 ears of corn
- Dumpling
- 3/4 cup flour
- 1/2 tsp baking powder
- 1/2 tsp salt
- 1/4 tsp black pepper
- 1 tbsp butter
- 1/4 cup whole milk

Instructions

Finely chop onion, garlic, celery stalk, carrot, red pepper and green pepper, set aside.

Melt butter in a deep pot, add all finely chopped vegetables and corn.

Add salt, black pepper, parsley, and thyme, saute for 1-2 minutes then add 3 cups water, bring to a low boil for 35-40 minutes.

Add more water 1/2 cup at a time if split peas still need to cook more.

Once split peas are completely soft, use a blender to puree soup.

Add coconut milk, 4 cups water, salt or bouillon cube, black pepper, and scotch bonnet if using. Stir and bring to a low boil, about 20-25 minutes.

Make dumplings. Mix dry dumpling ingredients together, rub butter in, add whole milk to knead and bring together to form a dough ball, set aside.

While soup boils, peel and chop plantains into 2 inches. If using fresh corn on the cob, chop into 4 inch pieces. Add corn kernels, corn ears, diced carrots, and plantains to soup. Break dumpling dough into pieces and drop into soup. Let vegetables and dumplings cook until plantains are cooked through.

Remove from heat and adjust salt and black pepper to taste.

Dhal

Ingredients

- 8 cups water
- 1/2 tsp masala
- 1/2 tsp curry powder
- 1/4 tsp tumeric
- 1/4 tsp ground geera
- 1 1/4 tsp salt
- 3/4 cup split peas

- 5 garlic cloves
- 1 whole onion
- 3 wiri wiri pepper
- 1 small tomato, optional
- 1 tsp whole cumin (geera) seeds
- 1 garlic thinly sliced

Instructions

Bring 8 cups of water to a rapid boil. Rinse split peas and add to the water.

Chop onion, garlic, tomato, and wiri wiri peppers (or scotch bonnet) and add to boiling water. Add spices and salt (I usually like a bit more salt in my food so start with 1 tsp and add more if needed).

Boil peas for 45 minutes until peas are soft to the touch. Blend with immersion blender or use swizzle stick to achieve a smooth texture. Return to a slow boil for another 15-20 minutes until dhal gets slightly thick. Turn heat off when you have reached your desired texture.

In a metal ladle or very small pot, heat oil and fry sliced garlic and geera until they become slightly burnt. Immediately add to dhal, being careful to cover the pot as you add the garlic/geera mixture as the hot oil will pitch out at you since it is being combined with a water based liquid.

Cow Heel Soup

A traditional soup made in the Caribbean. Full of yams, cassavas, potato and split peas simmered down with cow heel and salted pigtail.

INGREDIENTS

- 1 cup yellow split peas
- 1 1/2 lb cow heel
- 1 cup cubed pumpkin
- 1/2 medium onion, chopped
- 1/2 lb salted pigtail, cut up
- 2 cloves garlic
- 1 teaspoon black pepper
- 2 medium sweet potato, cubed
- 1 carrot, chopped
- 2 corn on the cob (chopped)
- Dumplings
- 3 cups water
- 1/4 cup chopped celery
- 1/4 cup chopped chive
- Salt and pepper to taste
- Water

INSTRUCTIONS

Wash cow heel and put to boil with the 3 cups of water

When boiling add onion, garlic, salt and cool until cow heel is tender

When tender, add split peas and cook for about 20 minutes

Add pigtails, and provisions (pumpkin, sweet potato, carrots, corn on the cob and any other provision that you may want to add)

Add celery and chive

Add dumplings and additional water. Enough to cover the items in the pot

Leave on medium low until provision is ready

Season to taste.

Split Peas Soup

Ingredients

- 1/2 pt split peas
- 1/2 oz fat for frying
- 1 onion, sliced
- a ham bone or bacon scraps
- 2 pt water or stock
- 8 oz eddoes or yam, diced

Instructions

Heat fat, and sauté onion lightly.

Add peas and fry lightly.

Add ham bone or scraps and stock and bring to simmering point.

Cook until peas are tender.

Add more water if soup seems too thick, then add the diced root vegetables and salt and pepper to taste. Simmer for a further 10 minutes.

Serve hot.

Shrimp And Callaloo Soup

Ingredients

- 1 oz shrimp or prawns
- 1 bundle callaloo or Bakchoy
- 1 large onion
- 1/2 oz fat for frying
- 2 pt water or stock
- eschalot
- celery
- soy sauce

Instructions

- Chop onion and saute lightly in hot fat.
- Add the water, and the eschalot and celery tied together.
- Season with white pepper and salt and bring to simmering point.
- Allow to simmer for about 30 minutes.
- Clean shrimps thoroughly and add to soup. Cook for 5 minutes.
- Add finely shredded callaloo or pakchoy. Simmer for a further 3
- minutes.
- Add a few drops of soy sauce.
- Serve hot.
-

West Indian Pepper Sauce

Ingredients

- 2lbs wiri wiri pepper or scotch bonnet peppers (stems removed)
- 1 green mango (unripe mango) or 2 large cucumbers, peeled and
- diced
- 1 head of garlic, peeled
- 2 tsp salt
- 1/2 cup white distilled vinegar

Directions

Rinse peppers and remove all stems

Add about 1 cup of peppers to a blender with a little mango or

cucumber, a little bit of vinegar and garlic, blend until smooth.

Repeat process until all ingredients are used up and sauce is

smooth and not watery (it should have a tomato/pasta sauce texture).

Store sauce in a mason jar.

Enjoy !!

www.ingramcontent.com/pod-product-compliance
Lightning Source LLC
Chambersburg PA
CBHW041124120626

46547CB00019B/2846

9781965732854